Welcome

The purpose.

I like setting goals, but it has taken me a while to make sure that I am on track daily. So this is where the 5 a day comes in. Just like us having our 5 a day of fruit and veg to keep us physically healthy, journaling, doing and celebrating 5 of our achievements a day can keep us spiritually healthy.

So here is a guide on how to use the book to it's best.

1. Write down the things you would like to achieve in the next 90 days (three months)

Use the headings: Family, work /career, Financial, Spiritual , and Personal

2. Decide on activities you need to be doing in order to meet these goals—these tasks can then go in the what I need to do today column. Note them down here.

3. Write down some of the things you have done—this will help you when you need to think about good things about yourself.

4. Are there any resources or people you need to help you with your goals? Write them in here.

5. Now you are ready to go and start using the planner.

Step 1. Think about 5 positive things about yourself and write them in column 1. Use your achievements list to help you to start with

Step 2. Using the activities towards your goals Write down 5 tasks you need to move towards the goals—Every journey starts with a single step. Tick them off as you accomplish them.

Step 3—At the end of the day, just before you finish for the day, write down 5 things that you have achieved and are grateful for.

Repeat on a daily basis for the next 90 days.

Join our Facebook group and share your journey…..

To your success…x *Susie xx*

Day _____   Date _____

Step 1. Write 5 things you like about yourself

1. _____

2. _____

3. _____

4. _____

5. _____

Say them out loud to yourself. Remember you are loved.

Step 2. Write down 5 things you would like to achieve today

1. _____

2. _____

3. _____

4. _____

5. _____

Awesome! Tick them off as you go.

Step 3. Write down 5 things you have achieved and/or grateful for today.

1. _____

2. _____

3. _____

4. _____

5. _____

Well done for achieving your goals. Remember it is small steps consistently which helps you to move forward.

Day _____ Date _____

Step 1. Write 5 things you like about yourself

1. _____

2. _____

3. _____

4. _____

5. _____

Say them out loud to yourself. Remember you are loved.

Step 2. Write down 5 things you would like to achieve today

1. _____

2. _____

3. _____

4. _____

5. _____

Awesome! Tick them off as you go.

Step 3. Write down 5 things you have achieved and/or grateful for today.

1. _____

2. _____

3. _____

4. _____

5. _____

Well done for achieving your goals. Remember it is small steps consistently which helps you to move forward.

Day _____   Date _____

Step 1. Write 5 things you like about yourself

1. _____

2. _____

3. _____

4. _____

5. _____

Say them out loud to yourself. Remember you are loved.

Step 2. Write down 5 things you would like to achieve today

1. _____

2. _____

3. _____

4. _____

5. _____

Awesome! Tick them off as you go.

Step 3. Write down 5 things you have achieved and/or grateful for today.

1. _____

2. _____

3. _____

4. _____

5. _____

Well done for achieving your goals. Remember it is small steps consistently which helps you to move forward.

Day _____ Date _____

Step 1. Write 5 things you like about yourself

1. _____

2. _____

3. _____

4. _____

5. _____

Say them out loud to yourself. Remember you are loved.

Step 2. Write down 5 things you would like to achieve today

1. _____

2. _____

3. _____

4. _____

5. _____

Awesome! Tick them off as you go.

Step 3. Write down 5 things you have achieved and/or grateful for today.

1. _____

2. _____

3. _____

4. _____

5. _____

Well done for achieving your goals. Remember it is small steps consistently which helps you to move forward.

Day _____   Date _____

Step 1. Write 5 things you like about yourself

1. _____

2. _____

3. _____

4. _____

5. _____

Say them out loud to yourself. Remember you are loved.

Step 2. Write down 5 things you would like to achieve today

1. _____

2. _____

3. _____

4. _____

5. _____

Awesome! Tick them off as you go.

Step 3. Write down 5 things you have achieved and/or grateful for today.

1. _____

2. _____

3. _____

4. _____

5. _____

Well done for achieving your goals. Remember it is small steps consistently which helps you to move forward.

Day _____ Date _____

Step 1. Write 5 things you like about yourself

1. _____

2. _____

3. _____

4. _____

5. _____

Say them out loud to yourself. Remember you are loved.

Step 2. Write down 5 things you would like to achieve today

1. _____

2. _____

3. _____

4. _____

5. _____

Awesome! Tick them off as you go.

Step 3. Write down 5 things you have achieved and/or grateful for today.

1. _____

2. _____

3. _____

4. _____

5. _____

Well done for achieving your goals. Remember it is small steps consistently which helps you to move forward.

Day _____   Date _____

Step 1. Write 5 things you like about yourself

1. _____

2. _____

3. _____

4. _____

5. _____

Say them out loud to yourself. Remember you are loved.

Step 2. Write down 5 things you would like to achieve today

1. _____

2. _____

3. _____

4. _____

5. _____

Awesome! Tick them off as you go.

Step 3. Write down 5 things you have achieved and/or grateful for today.

1. _____

2. _____

3. _____

4. _____

5. _____

Well done for achieving your goals. Remember it is small steps consistently which helps you to move forward.

Day _____   Date _____

Step 1. Write 5 things you like about yourself

1. _____

2. _____

3. _____

4. _____

5. _____

Say them out loud to yourself. Remember you are loved.

Step 2. Write down 5 things you would like to achieve today

1. _____

2. _____

3. _____

4. _____

5. _____

Awesome! Tick them off as you go.

Step 3. Write down 5 things you have achieved and/or grateful for today.

1. _____

2. _____

3. _____

4. _____

5. _____

Well done for achieving your goals. Remember it is small steps consistently which helps you to move forward.

Day _____   Date _____

Step 1. Write 5 things you like about yourself

1. _____

2. _____

3. _____

4. _____

5. _____

Say them out loud to yourself. Remember you are loved.

Step 2. Write down 5 things you would like to achieve today

1. _____

2. _____

3. _____

4. _____

5. _____

Awesome! Tick them off as you go.

Step 3. Write down 5 things you have achieved and/or grateful for today.

1. _____

2. _____

3. _____

4. _____

5. _____

Well done for achieving your goals. Remember it is small steps consistently which helps you to move forward.

Day _____ Date _____

Step 1. Write 5 things you like about yourself

1. _____

2. _____

3. _____

4. _____

5. _____

Say them out loud to yourself. Remember you are loved.

Step 2. Write down 5 things you would like to achieve today

1. _____

2. _____

3. _____

4. _____

5. _____

Awesome! Tick them off as you go.

Step 3. Write down 5 things you have achieved and/or grateful for today.

1. _____

2. _____

3. _____

4. _____

5. _____

Well done for achieving your goals. Remember it is small steps consistently which helps you to move forward.

Day _____   Date _____

Step 1. Write 5 things you like about yourself

1. _____

2. _____

3. _____

4. _____

5. _____

Say them out loud to yourself. Remember you are loved.

Step 2. Write down 5 things you would like to achieve today

1. _____

2. _____

3. _____

4. _____

5. _____

Awesome! Tick them off as you go.

Step 3. Write down 5 things you have achieved and/or grateful for today.

1. _____

2. _____

3. _____

4. _____

5. _____

Well done for achieving your goals. Remember it is small steps consistently which helps you to move forward.

Day   Date

Step 1. Write 5 things you like about yourself

1. _____

2. _____

3. _____

4. _____

5. _____

Say them out loud to yourself. Remember you are loved.

Step 2. Write down 5 things you would like to achieve today

1. _____

2. _____

3. _____

4. _____

5. _____

Awesome! Tick them off as you go.

Step 3. Write down 5 things you have achieved and/or grateful for today.

1._____

2._____

3._____

4. _____

5. _____

Well done for achieving your goals. Remember it is small steps consistently which helps you to move forward.

Day _____   Date _____

Step 1. Write 5 things you like about yourself

1. _____

2. _____

3. _____

4. _____

5. _____

Say them out loud to yourself. Remember you are loved.

Step 2. Write down 5 things you would like to achieve today

1. _____

2. _____

3. _____

4. _____

5. _____

Awesome! Tick them off as you go.

Step 3. Write down 5 things you have achieved and/or grateful for today.

1._____

2._____

3._____

4. _____

5. _____

Well done for achieving your goals. Remember it is small steps consistently which helps you to move forward.

Day   Date

Step 1. Write 5 things you like about yourself

1. _____

2. _____

3. _____

4. _____

5. _____

Say them out loud to yourself. Remember you are loved.

Step 2. Write down 5 things you would like to achieve today

1. _____

2. _____

3. _____

4. _____

5. _____

Awesome! Tick them off as you go.

Step 3. Write down 5 things you have achieved and/or grateful for today.

1._____

2._____

3._____

4. _____

5. _____

Well done for achieving your goals. Remember it is small steps consistently which helps you to move forward.

Day   Date

Step 1. Write 5 things you like about yourself

1. _____

2. _____

3. _____

4. _____

5. _____

Say them out loud to yourself. Remember you are loved.

Step 2. Write down 5 things you would like to achieve today

1. _____

2. _____

3. _____

4. _____

5. _____

Awesome! Tick them off as you go.

Step 3. Write down 5 things you have achieved and/or grateful for today.

1. _____

2. _____

3. _____

4. _____

5. _____

Well done for achieving your goals. Remember it is small steps consistently which helps you to move forward.

Day   Date

Step 1. Write 5 things you like about yourself

1. _____

2. _____

3. _____

4. _____

5. _____

Say them out loud to yourself. Remember you are loved.

Step 2. Write down 5 things you would like to achieve today

1. _____

2. _____

3. _____

4. _____

5. _____

Awesome! Tick them off as you go.

Step 3. Write down 5 things you have achieved and/or grateful for today.

1. _____

2. _____

3. _____

4. _____

5. _____

Well done for achieving your goals. Remember it is small steps consistently which helps you to move forward.

Day   Date

Step 1. Write 5 things you like about yourself

1. _____

2. _____

3. _____

4. _____

5. _____

Say them out loud to yourself. Remember you are loved.

Step 2. Write down 5 things you would like to achieve today

1. _____

2. _____

3. _____

4. _____

5. _____

Awesome! Tick them off as you go.

Step 3. Write down 5 things you have achieved and/or grateful for today.

1. _____

2. _____

3. _____

4. _____

5. _____

Well done for achieving your goals. Remember it is small steps consistently which helps you to move forward.

Step 1. Write 5 things you like about yourself

1. _____

2. _____

3. _____

4. _____

5. _____

Say them out loud to yourself. Remember you are loved.

Step 2. Write down 5 things you would like to achieve today

1. _____

2. _____

3. _____

4. _____

5. _____

Awesome! Tick them off as you go.

Step 3. Write down 5 things you have achieved and/or grateful for today.

1. _____

2. _____

3. _____

4. _____

5. _____

Well done for achieving your goals. Remember it is small steps consistently which helps you to move forward.

Day 19   Date _____

Step 1. Write 5 things you like about yourself

1. _____

2. _____

3. _____

4. _____

5. _____

Say them out loud to yourself. Remember you are loved.

Step 2. Write down 5 things you would like to achieve today

1. _____

2. _____

3. _____

4. _____

5. _____

Awesome! Tick them off as you go.

Step 3. Write down 5 things you have achieved and/or grateful for today.

1. _____

2. _____

3. _____

4. _____

5. _____

Well done for achieving your goals. Remember it is small steps consistently which helps you to move forward.

Day   Date

Step 1. Write 5 things you like about yourself

1. _____

2. _____

3. _____

4. _____

5. _____

Say them out loud to yourself. Remember you are loved.

Step 2. Write down 5 things you would like to achieve today

1. _____

2. _____

3. _____

4. _____

5. _____

Awesome! Tick them off as you go.

Step 3. Write down 5 things you have achieved and/or grateful for today.

1. _____

2. _____

3. _____

4. _____

5. _____

Well done for achieving your goals. Remember it is small steps consistently which helps you to move forward.

Day   Date

Step 1. Write 5 things you like about yourself

1. _____

2. _____

3. _____

4. _____

5. _____

Say them out loud to yourself. Remember you are loved.

Step 2. Write down 5 things you would like to achieve today

1. _____

2. _____

3. _____

4. _____

5. _____

Awesome! Tick them off as you go.

Step 3. Write down 5 things you have achieved and/or grateful for today.

1. _____

2. _____

3. _____

4. _____

5. _____

Well done for achieving your goals. Remember it is small steps consistently which helps you to move forward.

Day _____   Date _____

Step 1. Write 5 things you like about yourself

1. _____

2. _____

3. _____

4. _____

5. _____

Say them out loud to yourself. Remember you are loved.

Step 2. Write down 5 things you would like to achieve today

1. _____

2. _____

3. _____

4. _____

5. _____

Awesome! Tick them off as you go.

Step 3. Write down 5 things you have achieved and/or grateful for today.

1. _____

2. _____

3. _____

4. _____

5. _____

Well done for achieving your goals. Remember it is small steps consistently which helps you to move forward.

Day _____   Date _____

Step 1. Write 5 things you like about yourself

1. _____

2. _____

3. _____

4. _____

5. _____

Say them out loud to yourself. Remember you are loved.

Step 2. Write down 5 things you would like to achieve today

1. _____

2. _____

3. _____

4. _____

5. _____

Awesome! Tick them off as you go.

Step 3. Write down 5 things you have achieved and/or grateful for today.

1. _____

2. _____

3. _____

4. _____

5. _____

Well done for achieving your goals. Remember it is small steps consistently which helps you to move forward.

Day   Date

Step 1. Write 5 things you like about yourself

1. _____

2. _____

3. _____

4. _____

5. _____

Say them out loud to yourself. Remember you are loved.

Step 2. Write down 5 things you would like to achieve today

1. _____

2. _____

3. _____

4. _____

5. _____

Awesome! Tick them off as you go.

Step 3. Write down 5 things you have achieved and/or grateful for today.

1. _____

2. _____

3. _____

4. _____

5. _____

Well done for achieving your goals. Remember it is small steps consistently which helps you to move forward.

Day _____   Date _____

Step 1. Write 5 things you like about yourself

1. _____

2. _____

3. _____

4. _____

5. _____

Say them out loud to yourself. Remember you are loved.

Step 2. Write down 5 things you would like to achieve today

1. _____

2. _____

3. _____

4. _____

5. _____

Awesome! Tick them off as you go.

Step 3. Write down 5 things you have achieved and/or grateful for today.

1. _____

2. _____

3. _____

4. _____

5. _____

Well done for achieving your goals. Remember it is small steps consistently which helps you to move forward.

Day   Date

Step 1. Write 5 things you like about yourself

1. _____

2. _____

3. _____

4. _____

5. _____

Say them out loud to yourself. Remember you are loved.

Step 2. Write down 5 things you would like to achieve today

1. _____

2. _____

3. _____

4. _____

5. _____

Awesome! Tick them off as you go.

Step 3. Write down 5 things you have achieved and/or grateful for today.

1. _____

2. _____

3. _____

4. _____

5. _____

Well done for achieving your goals. Remember it is small steps consistently which helps you to move forward.

Day   Date

Step 1. Write 5 things you like about yourself

1. _____

2. _____

3. _____

4. _____

5. _____

Say them out loud to yourself. Remember you are loved.

Step 2. Write down 5 things you would like to achieve today

1. _____

2. _____

3. _____

4. _____

5. _____

Awesome! Tick them off as you go.

Step 3. Write down 5 things you have achieved and/or grateful for today.

1. _____

2. _____

3. _____

4. _____

5. _____

Well done for achieving your goals. Remember it is small steps consistently which helps you to move forward.

Day   Date

Step 1. Write 5 things you like about yourself

1. _____

2. _____

3. _____

4. _____

5. _____

Say them out loud to yourself. Remember you are loved.

Step 2. Write down 5 things you would like to achieve today

1. _____

2. _____

3. _____

4. _____

5. _____

Awesome! Tick them off as you go.

Step 3. Write down 5 things you have achieved and/or grateful for today.

1. _____

2. _____

3. _____

4. _____

5. _____

Well done for achieving your goals. Remember it is small steps consistently which helps you to move forward.

Day   Date

Step 1. Write 5 things you like about yourself

1. _____

2. _____

3. _____

4. _____

5. _____

Say them out loud to yourself. Remember you are loved.

Step 2. Write down 5 things you would like to achieve today

1. _____

2. _____

3. _____

4. _____

5. _____

Awesome! Tick them off as you go.

Step 3. Write down 5 things you have achieved and/or grateful for today.

1. _____

2. _____

3. _____

4. _____

5. _____

Well done for achieving your goals. Remember it is small steps consistently which helps you to move forward.

Day   Date

Step 1. Write 5 things you like about yourself

1. _____

2. _____

3. _____

4. _____

5. _____

Say them out loud to yourself. Remember you are loved.

Step 2. Write down 5 things you would like to achieve today

1. _____

2. _____

3. _____

4. _____

5. _____

Awesome! Tick them off as you go.

Step 3. Write down 5 things you have achieved and/or grateful for today.

1. _____

2. _____

3. _____

4. _____

5. _____

Well done for achieving your goals. Remember it is small steps consistently which helps you to move forward.

Day   Date

Step 1. Write 5 things you like about yourself

1. _____

2. _____

3. _____

4. _____

5. _____

Say them out loud to yourself. Remember you are loved.

Step 2. Write down 5 things you would like to achieve today

1. _____

2. _____

3. _____

4. _____

5. _____

Awesome! Tick them off as you go.

Step 3. Write down 5 things you have achieved and/or grateful for today.

1. _____

2. _____

3. _____

4. _____

5. _____

Well done for achieving your goals. Remember it is small steps consistently which helps you to move forward.

Day _____ Date _____

Step 1. Write 5 things you like about yourself

1. _____

2. _____

3. _____

4. _____

5. _____

Say them out loud to yourself. Remember you are loved.

Step 2. Write down 5 things you would like to achieve today

1. _____

2. _____

3. _____

4. _____

5. _____

Awesome! Tick them off as you go.

Step 3. Write down 5 things you have achieved and/or grateful for today.

1. _____

2. _____

3. _____

4. _____

5. _____

Well done for achieving your goals. Remember it is small steps consistently which helps you to move forward.

Day   Date _____

Step 1. Write 5 things you like about yourself

1. _____

2. _____

3. _____

4. _____

5. _____

Say them out loud to yourself. Remember you are loved.

Step 2. Write down 5 things you would like to achieve today

1. _____

2. _____

3. _____

4. _____

5. _____

Awesome! Tick them off as you go.

Step 3. Write down 5 things you have achieved and/or grateful for today.

1. _____

2. _____

3. _____

4. _____

5. _____

Well done for achieving your goals. Remember it is small steps consistently which helps you to move forward.

Day   Date _____

Step 1. Write 5 things you like about yourself

1. _____

2. _____

3. _____

4. _____

5. _____

Say them out loud to yourself. Remember you are loved.

Step 2. Write down 5 things you would like to achieve today

1. _____

2. _____

3. _____

4. _____

5. _____

Awesome! Tick them off as you go.

Step 3. Write down 5 things you have achieved and/or grateful for today.

1. _____

2. _____

3. _____

4. _____

5. _____

Well done for achieving your goals. Remember it is small steps consistently which helps you to move forward.

Day _____   Date _____

Step 1. Write 5 things you like about yourself

1. _____

2. _____

3. _____

4. _____

5. _____

Say them out loud to yourself. Remember you are loved.

Step 2. Write down 5 things you would like to achieve today

1. _____

2. _____

3. _____

4. _____

5. _____

Awesome! Tick them off as you go.

Step 3. Write down 5 things you have achieved and/or grateful for today.

1. _____

2. _____

3. _____

4. _____

5. _____

Well done for achieving your goals. Remember it is small steps consistently which helps you to move forward.

Day _____ Date _____

Step 1. Write 5 things you like about yourself

1. _____

2. _____

3. _____

4. _____

5. _____

Say them out loud to yourself. Remember you are loved.

Step 2. Write down 5 things you would like to achieve today

1. _____

2. _____

3. _____

4. _____

5. _____

Awesome! Tick them off as you go.

Step 3. Write down 5 things you have achieved and/or grateful for today.

1. _____

2. _____

3. _____

4. _____

5. _____

Well done for achieving your goals. Remember it is small steps consistently which helps you to move forward.

Day _____   Date _____

Step 1. Write 5 things you like about yourself

1. _____

2. _____

3. _____

4. _____

5. _____

Say them out loud to yourself. Remember you are loved.

Step 2. Write down 5 things you would like to achieve today

1. _____

2. _____

3. _____

4. _____

5. _____

Awesome! Tick them off as you go.

Step 3. Write down 5 things you have achieved and/or grateful for today.

1. _____

2. _____

3. _____

4. _____

5. _____

Well done for achieving your goals. Remember it is small steps consistently which helps you to move forward.

Day _____   Date _____

Step 1. Write 5 things you like about yourself

1. _____

2. _____

3. _____

4. _____

5. _____

Say them out loud to yourself. Remember you are loved.

Step 2. Write down 5 things you would like to achieve today

1. _____

2. _____

3. _____

4. _____

5. _____

Awesome! Tick them off as you go.

Step 3. Write down 5 things you have achieved and/or grateful for today.

1. _____

2. _____

3. _____

4. _____

5. _____

Well done for achieving your goals. Remember it is small steps consistently which helps you to move forward.

Day _____   Date _____

Step 1. Write 5 things you like about yourself

1. _____

2. _____

3. _____

4. _____

5. _____

Say them out loud to yourself. Remember you are loved.

Step 2. Write down 5 things you would like to achieve today

1. _____

2. _____

3. _____

4. _____

5. _____

Awesome! Tick them off as you go.

Step 3. Write down 5 things you have achieved and/or grateful for today.

1. _____

2. _____

3. _____

4. _____

5. _____

Well done for achieving your goals. Remember it is small steps consistently which helps you to move forward.

Day   Date _____

Step 1. Write 5 things you like about yourself

1. _____

2. _____

3. _____

4. _____

5. _____

Say them out loud to yourself. Remember you are loved.

Step 2. Write down 5 things you would like to achieve today

1. _____

2. _____

3. _____

4. _____

5. _____

Awesome! Tick them off as you go.

Step 3. Write down 5 things you have achieved and/or grateful for today.

1. _____

2. _____

3. _____

4. _____

5. _____

Well done for achieving your goals. Remember it is small steps consistently which helps you to move forward.

Day _____   Date _____

Step 1. Write 5 things you like about yourself

1. _____

2. _____

3. _____

4. _____

5. _____

Say them out loud to yourself. Remember you are loved.

Step 2. Write down 5 things you would like to achieve today

1. _____

2. _____

3. _____

4. _____

5. _____

Awesome! Tick them off as you go.

Step 3. Write down 5 things you have achieved and/or grateful for today.

1. _____

2. _____

3. _____

4. _____

5. _____

Well done for achieving your goals. Remember it is small steps consistently which helps you to move forward.

Day _____   Date _____

Step 1. Write 5 things you like about yourself

1. _____

2. _____

3. _____

4. _____

5. _____

Say them out loud to yourself. Remember you are loved.

Step 2. Write down 5 things you would like to achieve today

1. _____

2. _____

3. _____

4. _____

5. _____

Awesome! Tick them off as you go.

Step 3. Write down 5 things you have achieved and/or grateful for today.

1. _____

2. _____

3. _____

4. _____

5. _____

Well done for achieving your goals. Remember it is small steps consistently which helps you to move forward.

Day _____   Date _____

Step 1. Write 5 things you like about yourself

1. _____

2. _____

3. _____

4. _____

5. _____

Say them out loud to yourself. Remember you are loved.

Step 2. Write down 5 things you would like to achieve today

1. _____

2. _____

3. _____

4. _____

5. _____

Awesome! Tick them off as you go.

Step 3. Write down 5 things you have achieved and/or grateful for today.

1. _____

2. _____

3. _____

4. _____

5. _____

Well done for achieving your goals. Remember it is small steps consistently which helps you to move forward.

Day _____   Date _____

Step 1. Write 5 things you like about yourself

1. _____

2. _____

3. _____

4. _____

5. _____

Say them out loud to yourself. Remember you are loved.

Step 2. Write down 5 things you would like to achieve today

1. _____

2. _____

3. _____

4. _____

5. _____

Awesome! Tick them off as you go.

Step 3. Write down 5 things you have achieved and/or grateful for today.

1. _____

2. _____

3. _____

4. _____

5. _____

Well done for achieving your goals. Remember it is small steps consistently which helps you to move forward.

Day _____ Date _____

Step 1. Write 5 things you like about yourself

1. _____

2. _____

3. _____

4. _____

5. _____

Say them out loud to yourself. Remember you are loved.

Step 2. Write down 5 things you would like to achieve today

1. _____

2. _____

3. _____

4. _____

5. _____

Awesome! Tick them off as you go.

Step 3. Write down 5 things you have achieved and/or grateful for today.

1. _____

2. _____

3. _____

4. _____

5. _____

Well done for achieving your goals. Remember it is small steps consistently which helps you to move forward.

Day _____   Date _____

Step 1. Write 5 things you like about yourself

1. _____

2. _____

3. _____

4. _____

5. _____

Say them out loud to yourself. Remember you are loved.

Step 2. Write down 5 things you would like to achieve today

1. _____

2. _____

3. _____

4. _____

5. _____

Awesome! Tick them off as you go.

Step 3. Write down 5 things you have achieved and/or grateful for today.

1. _____

2. _____

3. _____

4. _____

5. _____

Well done for achieving your goals. Remember it is small steps consistently which helps you to move forward.

Day _____ Date _____

Step 1. Write 5 things you like about yourself

1. _____

2. _____

3. _____

4. _____

5. _____

Say them out loud to yourself. Remember you are loved.

Step 2. Write down 5 things you would like to achieve today

1. _____

2. _____

3. _____

4. _____

5. _____

Awesome! Tick them off as you go.

Step 3. Write down 5 things you have achieved and/or grateful for today.

1. _____

2. _____

3. _____

4. _____

5. _____

Well done for achieving your goals. Remember it is small steps consistently which helps you to move forward.

Day _____ Date _____

Step 1. Write 5 things you like about yourself

1. _____

2. _____

3. _____

4. _____

5. _____

Say them out loud to yourself. Remember you are loved.

Step 2. Write down 5 things you would like to achieve today

1. _____

2. _____

3. _____

4. _____

5. _____

Awesome! Tick them off as you go.

Step 3. Write down 5 things you have achieved and/or grateful for today.

1. _____

2. _____

3. _____

4. _____

5. _____

Well done for achieving your goals. Remember it is small steps consistently which helps you to move forward.

Day _____   Date _____

Step 1. Write 5 things you like about yourself

1. _____

2. _____

3. _____

4. _____

5. _____

Say them out loud to yourself. Remember you are loved.

Step 2. Write down 5 things you would like to achieve today

1. _____

2. _____

3. _____

4. _____

5. _____

Awesome! Tick them off as you go.

Step 3. Write down 5 things you have achieved and/or grateful for today.

1. _____

2. _____

3. _____

4. _____

5. _____

Well done for achieving your goals. Remember it is small steps consistently which helps you to move forward.

Day _____ Date _____

Step 1. Write 5 things you like about yourself

1. _____

2. _____

3. _____

4. _____

5. _____

Say them out loud to yourself. Remember you are loved.

Step 2. Write down 5 things you would like to achieve today

1. _____

2. _____

3. _____

4. _____

5. _____

Awesome! Tick them off as you go.

Step 3. Write down 5 things you have achieved and/or grateful for today.

1. _____

2. _____

3. _____

4. _____

5. _____

Well done for achieving your goals. Remember it is small steps consistently which helps you to move forward.

Day _____   Date _____

Step 1. Write 5 things you like about yourself

1. _____

2. _____

3. _____

4. _____

5. _____

Say them out loud to yourself. Remember you are loved.

Step 2. Write down 5 things you would like to achieve today

1. _____

2. _____

3. _____

4. _____

5. _____

Awesome! Tick them off as you go.

Step 3. Write down 5 things you have achieved and/or grateful for today.

1. _____

2. _____

3. _____

4. _____

5. _____

Well done for achieving your goals. Remember it is small steps consistently which helps you to move forward.

Day   Date _____

Step 1. Write 5 things you like about yourself

1. _____

2. _____

3. _____

4. _____

5. _____

Say them out loud to yourself. Remember you are loved.

Step 2. Write down 5 things you would like to achieve today

1. _____

2. _____

3. _____

4. _____

5. _____

Awesome! Tick them off as you go.

Step 3. Write down 5 things you have achieved and/or grateful for today.

1. _____

2. _____

3. _____

4. _____

5. _____

Well done for achieving your goals. Remember it is small steps consistently which helps you to move forward.

Day _____ Date _____

Step 1. Write 5 things you like about yourself

1. _____

2. _____

3. _____

4. _____

5. _____

Say them out loud to yourself. Remember you are loved.

Step 2. Write down 5 things you would like to achieve today

1. _____

2. _____

3. _____

4. _____

5. _____

Awesome! Tick them off as you go.

Step 3. Write down 5 things you have achieved and/or grateful for today.

1. _____

2. _____

3. _____

4. _____

5. _____

Well done for achieving your goals. Remember it is small steps consistently which helps you to move forward.

Day _____ Date _____

Step 1. Write 5 things you like about yourself

1. _____

2. _____

3. _____

4. _____

5. _____

Say them out loud to yourself. Remember you are loved.

Step 2. Write down 5 things you would like to achieve today

1. _____

2. _____

3. _____

4. _____

5. _____

Awesome! Tick them off as you go.

Step 3. Write down 5 things you have achieved and/or grateful for today.

1. _____

2. _____

3. _____

4. _____

5. _____

Well done for achieving your goals. Remember it is small steps consistently which helps you to move forward.

Day _____ Date _____

Step 1. Write 5 things you like about yourself

1. _____

2. _____

3. _____

4. _____

5. _____

Say them out loud to yourself. Remember you are loved.

Step 2. Write down 5 things you would like to achieve today

1. _____

2. _____

3. _____

4. _____

5. _____

Awesome! Tick them off as you go.

Step 3. Write down 5 things you have achieved and/or grateful for today.

1. _____

2. _____

3. _____

4. _____

5. _____

Well done for achieving your goals. Remember it is small steps consistently which helps you to move forward.

Day _____   Date _____

Step 1. Write 5 things you like about yourself

1. _____

2. _____

3. _____

4. _____

5. _____

Say them out loud to yourself. Remember you are loved.

Step 2. Write down 5 things you would like to achieve today

1. _____

2. _____

3. _____

4. _____

5. _____

Awesome! Tick them off as you go.

Step 3. Write down 5 things you have achieved and/or grateful for today.

1._____

2._____

3._____

4. _____

5. _____

Well done for achieving your goals. Remember it is small steps consistently which helps you to move forward.

Day _____   Date _____

Step 1. Write 5 things you like about yourself

1. _____

2. _____

3. _____

4. _____

5. _____

Say them out loud to yourself. Remember you are loved.

Step 2. Write down 5 things you would like to achieve today

1. _____

2. _____

3. _____

4. _____

5. _____

Awesome! Tick them off as you go.

Step 3. Write down 5 things you have achieved and/or grateful for today.

1. _____

2. _____

3. _____

4. _____

5. _____

Well done for achieving your goals. Remember it is small steps consistently which helps you to move forward.

Day   Date _____

Step 1. Write 5 things you like about yourself

1. _____

2. _____

3. _____

4. _____

5. _____

Say them out loud to yourself. Remember you are loved.

Step 2. Write down 5 things you would like to achieve today

1. _____

2. _____

3. _____

4. _____

5. _____

Awesome! Tick them off as you go.

Step 3. Write down 5 things you have achieved and/or grateful for today.

1. _____

2. _____

3. _____

4. _____

5. _____

Well done for achieving your goals. Remember it is small steps consistently which helps you to move forward.

Day _____   Date _____

Step 1. Write 5 things you like about yourself

1. _____

2. _____

3. _____

4. _____

5. _____

Say them out loud to yourself. Remember you are loved.

Step 2. Write down 5 things you would like to achieve today

1. _____

2. _____

3. _____

4. _____

5. _____

Awesome! Tick them off as you go.

Step 3. Write down 5 things you have achieved and/or grateful for today.

1. _____

2. _____

3. _____

4. _____

5. _____

Well done for achieving your goals. Remember it is small steps consistently which helps you to move forward.

Day _____   Date _____

Step 1. Write 5 things you like about yourself

1. _____

2. _____

3. _____

4. _____

5. _____

Say them out loud to yourself. Remember you are loved.

Step 2. Write down 5 things you would like to achieve today

1. _____

2. _____

3. _____

4. _____

5. _____

Awesome! Tick them off as you go.

Step 3. Write down 5 things you have achieved and/or grateful for today.

1. _____

2. _____

3. _____

4. _____

5. _____

Well done for achieving your goals. Remember it is small steps consistently which helps you to move forward.

Day _____   Date _____

Step 1. Write 5 things you like about yourself

1. _____

2. _____

3. _____

4. _____

5. _____

Say them out loud to yourself. Remember you are loved.

Step 2. Write down 5 things you would like to achieve today

1. _____

2. _____

3. _____

4. _____

5. _____

Awesome! Tick them off as you go.

Step 3. Write down 5 things you have achieved and/or grateful for today.

1. _____

2. _____

3. _____

4. _____

5. _____

Well done for achieving your goals. Remember it is small steps consistently which helps you to move forward.

Day _____   Date _____

Step 1. Write 5 things you like about yourself

1. _____

2. _____

3. _____

4. _____

5. _____

Say them out loud to yourself. Remember you are loved.

Step 2. Write down 5 things you would like to achieve today

1. _____

2. _____

3. _____

4. _____

5. _____

Awesome! Tick them off as you go.

Step 3. Write down 5 things you have achieved and/or grateful for today.

1. _____

2. _____

3. _____

4. _____

5. _____

Well done for achieving your goals. Remember it is small steps consistently which helps you to move forward.

Day _____   Date _____

Step 1. Write 5 things you like about yourself

1. _____

2. _____

3. _____

4. _____

5. _____

Say them out loud to yourself. Remember you are loved.

Step 2. Write down 5 things you would like to achieve today

1. _____

2. _____

3. _____

4. _____

5. _____

Awesome! Tick them off as you go.

Step 3. Write down 5 things you have achieved and/or grateful for today.

1. _____

2. _____

3. _____

4. _____

5. _____

Well done for achieving your goals. Remember it is small steps consistently which helps you to move forward.

Day _____   Date _____

Step 1. Write 5 things you like about yourself

1. _____

2. _____

3. _____

4. _____

5. _____

Say them out loud to yourself. Remember you are loved.

Step 2. Write down 5 things you would like to achieve today

1. _____

2. _____

3. _____

4. _____

5. _____

Awesome! Tick them off as you go.

Step 3. Write down 5 things you have achieved and/or grateful for today.

1. _____

2. _____

3. _____

4. _____

5. _____

Well done for achieving your goals. Remember it is small steps consistently which helps you to move forward.

Day _____ Date _____

Step 1. Write 5 things you like about yourself

1. _____

2. _____

3. _____

4. _____

5. _____

Say them out loud to yourself. Remember you are loved.

Step 2. Write down 5 things you would like to achieve today

1. _____

2. _____

3. _____

4. _____

5. _____

Awesome! Tick them off as you go.

Step 3. Write down 5 things you have achieved and/or grateful for today.

1. _____

2. _____

3. _____

4. _____

5. _____

Well done for achieving your goals. Remember it is small steps consistently which helps you to move forward.

Day _____ Date _____

Step 1. Write 5 things you like about yourself

1. _____

2. _____

3. _____

4. _____

5. _____

Say them out loud to yourself. Remember you are loved.

Step 2. Write down 5 things you would like to achieve today

1. _____

2. _____

3. _____

4. _____

5. _____

Awesome! Tick them off as you go.

Step 3. Write down 5 things you have achieved and/or grateful for today.

1. _____

2. _____

3. _____

4. _____

5. _____

Well done for achieving your goals. Remember it is small steps consistently which helps you to move forward.

Day _____ Date _____

Step 1. Write 5 things you like about yourself

1. _____

2. _____

3. _____

4. _____

5. _____

Say them out loud to yourself. Remember you are loved.

Step 2. Write down 5 things you would like to achieve today

1. _____

2. _____

3. _____

4. _____

5. _____

Awesome! Tick them off as you go.

Step 3. Write down 5 things you have achieved and/or grateful for today.

1. _____

2. _____

3. _____

4. _____

5. _____

Well done for achieving your goals. Remember it is small steps consistently which helps you to move forward.

Day _____   Date _____

Step 1. Write 5 things you like about yourself

1. _____

2. _____

3. _____

4. _____

5. _____

Say them out loud to yourself. Remember you are loved.

Step 2. Write down 5 things you would like to achieve today

1. _____

2. _____

3. _____

4. _____

5. _____

Awesome! Tick them off as you go.

Step 3. Write down 5 things you have achieved and/or grateful for today.

1. _____

2. _____

3. _____

4. _____

5. _____

Well done for achieving your goals. Remember it is small steps consistently which helps you to move forward.

Day _____   Date _____

Step 1. Write 5 things you like about yourself

1. _____

2. _____

3. _____

4. _____

5. _____

Say them out loud to yourself. Remember you are loved.

Step 2. Write down 5 things you would like to achieve today

1. _____

2. _____

3. _____

4. _____

5. _____

Awesome! Tick them off as you go.

Step 3. Write down 5 things you have achieved and/or grateful for today.

1. _____

2. _____

3. _____

4. _____

5. _____

Well done for achieving your goals. Remember it is small steps consistently which helps you to move forward.

Day _____   Date _____

Step 1. Write 5 things you like about yourself

1. _____

2. _____

3. _____

4. _____

5. _____

Say them out loud to yourself. Remember you are loved.

Step 2. Write down 5 things you would like to achieve today

1. _____

2. _____

3. _____

4. _____

5. _____

Awesome! Tick them off as you go.

Step 3. Write down 5 things you have achieved and/or grateful for today.

1. _____

2. _____

3. _____

4. _____

5. _____

Well done for achieving your goals. Remember it is small steps consistently which helps you to move forward.

Day _____ Date _____

Step 1. Write 5 things you like about yourself

1. _____

2. _____

3. _____

4. _____

5. _____

Say them out loud to yourself. Remember you are loved.

Step 2. Write down 5 things you would like to achieve today

1. _____

2. _____

3. _____

4. _____

5. _____

Awesome! Tick them off as you go.

Step 3. Write down 5 things you have achieved and/or grateful for today.

1. _____

2. _____

3. _____

4. _____

5. _____

Well done for achieving your goals. Remember it is small steps consistently which helps you to move forward.

Day _____   Date _____

Step 1. Write 5 things you like about yourself

1. _____

2. _____

3. _____

4. _____

5. _____

Say them out loud to yourself. Remember you are loved.

Step 2. Write down 5 things you would like to achieve today

1. _____

2. _____

3. _____

4. _____

5. _____

Awesome! Tick them off as you go.

Step 3. Write down 5 things you have achieved and/or grateful for today.

1. _____

2. _____

3. _____

4. _____

5. _____

Well done for achieving your goals. Remember it is small steps consistently which helps you to move forward.

Day _____   Date _____

Step 1. Write 5 things you like about yourself

1. _____

2. _____

3. _____

4. _____

5. _____

Say them out loud to yourself. Remember you are loved.

Step 2. Write down 5 things you would like to achieve today

1. _____

2. _____

3. _____

4. _____

5. _____

Awesome! Tick them off as you go.

Step 3. Write down 5 things you have achieved and/or grateful for today.

1. _____

2. _____

3. _____

4. _____

5. _____

Well done for achieving your goals. Remember it is small steps consistently which helps you to move forward.

Day _____   Date _____

Step 1. Write 5 things you like about yourself

1. _____

2. _____

3. _____

4. _____

5. _____

Say them out loud to yourself. Remember you are loved.

Step 2. Write down 5 things you would like to achieve today

1. _____

2. _____

3. _____

4. _____

5. _____

Awesome! Tick them off as you go.

Step 3. Write down 5 things you have achieved and/or grateful for today.

1. _____

2. _____

3. _____

4. _____

5. _____

Well done for achieving your goals. Remember it is small steps consistently which helps you to move forward.

Day _____   Date _____

Step 1. Write 5 things you like about yourself

1. _____

2. _____

3. _____

4. _____

5. _____

Say them out loud to yourself. Remember you are loved.

Step 2. Write down 5 things you would like to achieve today

1. _____

2. _____

3. _____

4. _____

5. _____

Awesome! Tick them off as you go.

Step 3. Write down 5 things you have achieved and/or grateful for today.

1. _____

2. _____

3. _____

4. _____

5. _____

Well done for achieving your goals. Remember it is small steps consistently which helps you to move forward.

Day _____   Date _____

Step 1. Write 5 things you like about yourself

1. _____

2. _____

3. _____

4. _____

5. _____

Say them out loud to yourself. Remember you are loved.

Step 2. Write down 5 things you would like to achieve today

1. _____

2. _____

3. _____

4. _____

5. _____

Awesome! Tick them off as you go.

Step 3. Write down 5 things you have achieved and/or grateful for today.

1. _____

2. _____

3. _____

4. _____

5. _____

Well done for achieving your goals. Remember it is small steps consistently which helps you to move forward.

Day _____ Date _____

Step 1. Write 5 things you like about yourself

1. _____

2. _____

3. _____

4. _____

5. _____

Say them out loud to yourself. Remember you are loved.

Step 2. Write down 5 things you would like to achieve today

1. _____

2. _____

3. _____

4. _____

5. _____

Awesome! Tick them off as you go.

Step 3. Write down 5 things you have achieved and/or grateful for today.

1. _____

2. _____

3. _____

4. _____

5. _____

Well done for achieving your goals. Remember it is small steps consistently which helps you to move forward.

Day _____   Date _____

Step 1. Write 5 things you like about yourself

1. _____

2. _____

3. _____

4. _____

5. _____

Say them out loud to yourself. Remember you are loved.

Step 2. Write down 5 things you would like to achieve today

1. _____

2. _____

3. _____

4. _____

5. _____

Awesome! Tick them off as you go.

Step 3. Write down 5 things you have achieved and/or grateful for today.

1. _____

2. _____

3. _____

4. _____

5. _____

Well done for achieving your goals. Remember it is small steps consistently which helps you to move forward.

Day _____   Date _____

Step 1. Write 5 things you like about yourself

1. _____

2. _____

3. _____

4. _____

5. _____

Say them out loud to yourself. Remember you are loved.

Step 2. Write down 5 things you would like to achieve today

1. _____

2. _____

3. _____

4. _____

5. _____

Awesome! Tick them off as you go.

Step 3. Write down 5 things you have achieved and/or grateful for today.

1. _____

2. _____

3. _____

4. _____

5. _____

Well done for achieving your goals. Remember it is small steps consistently which helps you to move forward.

Day _____ Date _____

Step 1. Write 5 things you like about yourself

1. _____

2. _____

3. _____

4. _____

5. _____

Say them out loud to yourself. Remember you are loved.

Step 2. Write down 5 things you would like to achieve today

1. _____

2. _____

3. _____

4. _____

5. _____

Awesome! Tick them off as you go.

Step 3. Write down 5 things you have achieved and/or grateful for today.

1. _____

2. _____

3. _____

4. _____

5. _____

Well done for achieving your goals. Remember it is small steps consistently which helps you to move forward.

Day   Date _____

Step 1. Write 5 things you like about yourself

1. _____

2. _____

3. _____

4. _____

5. _____

Say them out loud to yourself. Remember you are loved.

Step 2. Write down 5 things you would like to achieve today

1. _____

2. _____

3. _____

4. _____

5. _____

Awesome! Tick them off as you go.

Step 3. Write down 5 things you have achieved and/or grateful for today.

1. _____

2. _____

3. _____

4. _____

5. _____

Well done for achieving your goals. Remember it is small steps consistently which helps you to move forward.

Day _____   Date _____

Step 1. Write 5 things you like about yourself

1. _____

2. _____

3. _____

4. _____

5. _____

Say them out loud to yourself. Remember you are loved.

Step 2. Write down 5 things you would like to achieve today

1. _____

2. _____

3. _____

4. _____

5. _____

Awesome! Tick them off as you go.

Step 3. Write down 5 things you have achieved and/or grateful for today.

1. _____

2. _____

3. _____

4. _____

5. _____

Well done for achieving your goals. Remember it is small steps consistently which helps you to move forward.

Day _____   Date _____

Step 1. Write 5 things you like about yourself

1. _____

2. _____

3. _____

4. _____

5. _____

Say them out loud to yourself. Remember you are loved.

Step 2. Write down 5 things you would like to achieve today

1. _____

2. _____

3. _____

4. _____

5. _____

Awesome! Tick them off as you go.

Step 3. Write down 5 things you have achieved and/or grateful for today.

1. _____

2. _____

3. _____

4. _____

5. _____

Well done for achieving your goals. Remember it is small steps consistently which helps you to move forward.

Day _____   Date _____

Step 1. Write 5 things you like about yourself

1. _____

2. _____

3. _____

4. _____

5. _____

Say them out loud to yourself. Remember you are loved.

Step 2. Write down 5 things you would like to achieve today

1. _____

2. _____

3. _____

4. _____

5. _____

Awesome! Tick them off as you go.

Step 3. Write down 5 things you have achieved and/or grateful for today.

1. _____

2. _____

3. _____

4. _____

5. _____

Well done for achieving your goals. Remember it is small steps consistently which helps you to move forward.

Day _____ Date _____

Step 1. Write 5 things you like about yourself

1. _____

2. _____

3. _____

4. _____

5. _____

Say them out loud to yourself. Remember you are loved.

Step 2. Write down 5 things you would like to achieve today

1. _____

2. _____

3. _____

4. _____

5. _____

Awesome! Tick them off as you go.

Step 3. Write down 5 things you have achieved and/or grateful for today.

1. _____

2. _____

3. _____

4. _____

5. _____

Well done for achieving your goals. Remember it is small steps consistently which helps you to move forward.

Day _____   Date _____

Step 1. Write 5 things you like about yourself

1. _____

2. _____

3. _____

4. _____

5. _____

Say them out loud to yourself. Remember you are loved.

Step 2. Write down 5 things you would like to achieve today

1. _____

2. _____

3. _____

4. _____

5. _____

Awesome! Tick them off as you go.

Step 3. Write down 5 things you have achieved and/or grateful for today.

1. _____

2. _____

3. _____

4. _____

5. _____

Well done for achieving your goals. Remember it is small steps consistently which helps you to move forward.

Day _____   Date _____

Step 1. Write 5 things you like about yourself

1. _____

2. _____

3. _____

4. _____

5. _____

Say them out loud to yourself. Remember you are loved.

Step 2. Write down 5 things you would like to achieve today

1. _____

2. _____

3. _____

4. _____

5. _____

Awesome! Tick them off as you go.

Step 3. Write down 5 things you have achieved and/or grateful for today.

1. _____

2. _____

3. _____

4. _____

5. _____

Well done for achieving your goals. Remember it is small steps consistently which helps you to move forward.

Day _____   Date _____

Step 1. Write 5 things you like about yourself

1. _____

2. _____

3. _____

4. _____

5. _____

Say them out loud to yourself. Remember you are loved.

Step 2. Write down 5 things you would like to achieve today

1. _____

2. _____

3. _____

4. _____

5. _____

Awesome! Tick them off as you go.

Step 3. Write down 5 things you have achieved and/or grateful for today.

1. _____

2. _____

3. _____

4. _____

5. _____

Well done for achieving your goals. Remember it is small steps consistently which helps you to move forward.

Day _____   Date _____

Step 1. Write 5 things you like about yourself

1. _____

2. _____

3. _____

4. _____

5. _____

Say them out loud to yourself. Remember you are loved.

Step 2. Write down 5 things you would like to achieve today

1. _____

2. _____

3. _____

4. _____

5. _____

Awesome! Tick them off as you go.

Step 3. Write down 5 things you have achieved and/or grateful for today.

1. _____

2. _____

3. _____

4. _____

5. _____

Well done for achieving your goals. Remember it is small steps consistently which helps you to move forward.

Day _____   Date _____

Step 1. Write 5 things you like about yourself

1. _____

2. _____

3. _____

4. _____

5. _____

Say them out loud to yourself. Remember you are loved.

Step 2. Write down 5 things you would like to achieve today

1. _____

2. _____

3. _____

4. _____

5. _____

Awesome! Tick them off as you go.

Step 3. Write down 5 things you have achieved and/or grateful for today.

1. _____

2. _____

3. _____

4. _____

5. _____

Well done for achieving your goals. Remember it is small steps consistently which helps you to move forward.

www.ingramcontent.com/pod-product-compliance
Lightning Source LLC
Chambersburg PA
CBHW021452210526
45463CB00002B/756